Meet the Overs and the Unders

Making Sense of Sensory Processing

Jackie Brown, OTR/L

An Activity Book to Help Children Understand Their Sensory Needs

6448 Vista Dr.
Shawnee, KS 66218
www.aapcpublishing.com

Publisher's Cataloging-In-Publication

Names: Brown, Jackie (Jaclyn), author.

Title: Meet the Overs and the Unders : making sense of sensory processing : an activity book to help children understand their sensory needs / Jackie Brown.

Description: Audience: Elementary school-age children with the help of an adult.

Identifiers: ISBN: 9781942197478 (paperback) | 9781942197485 (ebook)

Subjects: LCSH: Sensory evaluation--Juvenile fiction. | Senses and sensation in children--Evaluation--Juvenile fiction. | Sensory disorders in children--Treatment. | Sensory integration dysfunction in children--Treatment. | Autism spectrum disorders in children--Treatment. | Interoception-- Problems, exercises, etc. | Sensorimotor integration--Problems, exercises, etc. | CYAC: Senses and sensation--Fiction. | LCGFT: Activity books. | Problems and exercises.

Classification: LCC: BF723.S75 B76 2019 | DDC: 155.4/189042--23

Introduction

As an occupational therapist (OT) for many years I have found it challenging to talk to children about sensory processing. One of the hardest parts is finding a simple definition and way to discuss an important process of our body that helps us complete things we do every day.

There are 8 senses: vestibular (balance to move), visual (eyes to look), auditory (ears to listen), tactile (skin to touch), olfactory (nose to smell), gustatory (mouth to taste), proprioceptive (muscles to sense body and objects around), and interoception (organs to feel). They help us understand what is happening around us and keep us comfortable and safe. The brain is in control of letting the body know what information is important and how to respond.

Sensory processing is the brain process of taking sensory input (i.e. touch) from the world around us, paying attention to the information (orientation), figuring out the message and determining whether the information is important (integration), and acting or reacting to the messages received (response).

For example, if something touches you, your skin first needs to notice you have been touched (register), then send a message to your brain. Your brain then needs to pay attention and locate what happened (orient), such as something touched you. Next your brain needs to figure out if it is important or not (integrate), such as something poking you like a rock in your shoe. Finally, your brain sends messages to the rest of your body telling it what to do next (respond), such as taking the rock out of your shoe.

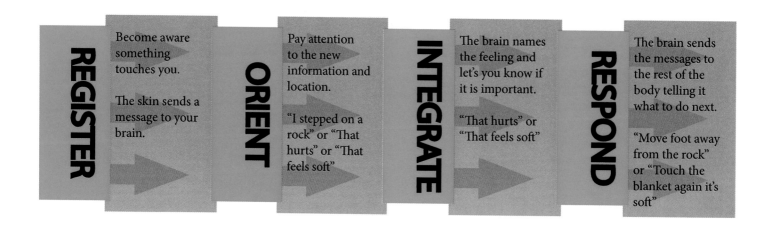

As a clinician I have found the most important part of addressing sensory challenges is to first identify whether a child is over-responsive or under-responsive.

Over-responsive (or over-reactive) individuals need LESS sensory information than most others. For example, if too many things are going on around them, they may try to run, hide or have a meltdown.

Under-responsive (or under-reactive) individuals need MORE sensory information than most others. For example, they may not respond if their name is called or notice when they bump into someone else.

Discovering whether someone is over- or under-responsive helps determine what sensory tools will best meet their sensory needs to help them feel more comfortable and confident.

I wrote this book to create an interactive tool to help parents, therapists, teachers, and other professionals find a child-friendly format to provide education on sensory issues. For parents, I highly recommend finding and working with a qualified professional trained in sensory processing to identify your child's specific sensory patterns and sensory tools to help support their nervous system.

I hope this book gives all of you a way to more easily communicate with the children in your life who have sensory issues and to figure out if they are more like the Overs or the Unders.

Thank you to my family, friends, and the children I work with who inspire me each day.

Jackie Brown, OTR/L

Meet the Overs.

They are over-responsive to sensory input.

This means they need LESS input to their body and brain than most people to meet their sensory needs.

They love it slow, dim, quiet, smooth, odor-free, bland, and gentle.

Meet the Unders.

They are under-responsive to sensory input.

This means they need MORE input to their body and brain than most people to meet their sensory needs.

They love it fast, bright, loud, bumpy, scented, spicy, and rough.

Every day we move.
We use our sense of balance to move.
It helps us to stand up, get around the house,
and play at recess.

The Overs
usually don't like to
move much. Most of the
time they like to sit, watch tv,
and play quietly.
They love to go slow.

The Unders
usually don't like
to sit still for long.
Most of the time they like to
run, jump, climb, and ride.
They love to go fast.

Who is more like you?
(Circle one)

This is how I am!

Every day we look.
We use our eyes to look.
Our eyes help us read, watch TV, draw and color.

The Overs
usually don't like bright lights.
Most of the time they like to
read, color, and draw, but with
the lights down low.
They love it dim.

The Unders
usually don't like dim lights or
bland, neutral colors. Most of the
time they like loud colors, pattern
fast-moving cartoons, and
videos games. They love it bright.

Who is more like you?
(Circle one)

This is how I see!

Every day we listen.
We use our ears to listen.
Our ears help us hear our friends and music.

The Overs usually don't like loud noises such as the vacuum, fireworks or big, noisy crowds. Most of the time they like to have soft music and sing to themselves to block out other sounds. They love it quiet.

The Unders usually don't like it too quiet. Most of the time they like playing loud games and having music on around them. They love it loud.

7

Who is more like you?
(Circle one)

This is how I hear!

Every day we touch.
We use our skin to touch.
Our skin helps us feel our clothes,
find things in the bottom of a drawer, and pet animals.

The Overs usually don't like things rough or scratchy, like crinkles in socks and tags on shirts. Most of the time they like things that are familiar, soft, and snuggly. Most often, they love things that are smooth.

The Unders usually don't care if their socks are twisted or their shoes are on the wrong feet. Most of the time they like things that are ooey, gooey, pokey, stretchy, and rough. They love things bumpy.

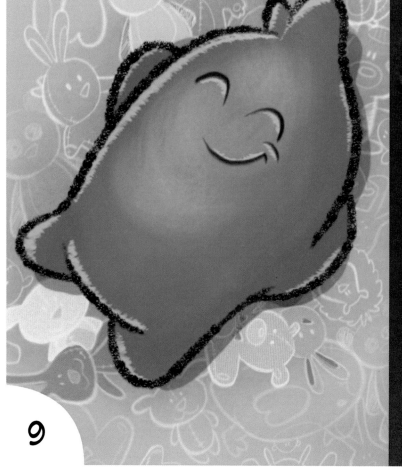

Who is more like you?
(Circle one)

This is how I feel!

Every day we smell.
We use our nose to smell.
Our nose helps us smell a flower
and know when dinner's ready.

The Overs usually don't like things with strong smells. Most of the time they like smells to be plain and gentle, such as warm cookies or a favorite shirt. They love things to be odor-free.

The Unders usually don't like things with soft or no smells. Most of the time they like strong smells, such as flowers, candles, scented lip balm, and perfumes. They love things to be scented.

11

Who is more like you?
(Circle one)

This is how I smell!

Every day we taste.
We use our mouth to taste.
Our mouth helps us find our favorite flavors
like spicy, sour, savory, and sweet.

The Overs usually don't like to try new foods. Most of the time they like familiar foods and want to eat the same things. They love their food bland.

The Unders usually don't like to eat boring food. Most of the time they like food with big flavors, such as salty, sweet, and sour. They love food spicy.

Who is more like you?
(Circle one)

This is how I taste!

Every day we sense our body and muscles.
We use our muscles and joints to sense
where our body is in comparison to objects around us.
It helps us not fall down, stay in our own space,
and play sports.

The Overs usually don't like to play rough. Most of the time they like slow, deep squeezes and burying themselves under things like pillows, cushions and blankets. They love to play gentle.

The Unders usually don't like to play slow and gentle. Most of the time they like to bounce, climb, tug, and pull. They love to play rough.

Who is more like you?
(Circle one)

This is how I play!

Every day we feel what is going on with our organs
(and your skin is your largest organ!).
Our organs tell us how we feel.
They help us feel pain, temperature,
when to use the bathroom, hunger, itches, and thirst.

The Overs are usually very aware of what is going on with their body. They are sometimes distracted or may act strongly when they are hungry, need to use the bathroom, or have pain. They are very aware of the feelings from their organs.

The Unders are usually less aware of what is going on with their body. They may not notice things, such as being hot or cold, when they are full after a meal, when they have a sore or when they need to use the bathroom. They are less aware of feelings from their organs.

Who is more like you?
(Circle one)

This is how my body feels!

When the Overs get
too much sensory input they
might have a meltdown
or shutdown. Not meeting
their sensory needs
can make things hard.

When the Unders don't get
enough sensory input they
might have a meltdown
or shutdown. Not meeting
their sensory needs
can make things hard.

19

Both the Overs and the Unders
are trying to meet their sensory needs,
but they don't know what to do.
They are having a hard time focusing,
following rules, and getting along with others.

What do you think
they can do?

Made in the USA
Middletown, DE
20 September 2021